Recorder Duets
from the Beginning

John Pitts

GW00658345

Duet playing brings extra pleasure to all involved, and with it an incentive to learn new notes and rhythms in order to succeed. A simultaneous development of listening skills and concentration is also required for successful ensemble playing.

Recorder Duets from the Beginning Books 1, 2 and *3* provide a wide range of repertoire to encourage duet playing by descant recorder players, both accompanied and unaccompanied. All the items are carefully graded, both in range of notes (pitches) included and in the level of difficulty. It is expected that players using Book 3 will have already reached the end of *Recorder from the Beginning Book 2* and started *Book 3*, in the author's widely popular teaching scheme.

The Pupil's Books include guitar chord symbols, and the Latin American items have suggestions for use of percussion instruments. The Teacher's Books include piano accompaniments for all the duets as well as the Latin American percussion parts.

In keeping with the 'repertoire' nature of the books, only a minimum of teaching help or explanation is given. Where more help is required it is best to refer to the appropriate pages of the teaching scheme *Recorder from the Beginning*.

Chester Music Limited
(A division of Music Sales Limited)
8/9 Frith Street, London W1V 5TZ

This book © Copyright 1996 Chester Music.
Order No. CH61253 ISBN 0-7119-6142-5

Music processed by Stave Origination.
Cover photography by Patrick Harrison.
Cover design by Jon Forss.
Printed in the United Kingdom by Caligraving Limited, Thetford, Norfolk.

Contents

To a Wild Rose   Edward MacDowell

2 = optional alternative fingering

Andante Grazioso   Mozart

Soldier's March   Schumann

Beckett Blues   Pitts

9

Polovtsian Dances   Borodin

At a moderate speed

Summertime   George Gershwin

Written in collaboration with DuBose and Dorothy Heyward and Ira Gershwin.

Largo   Corelli

Arcangelo **Corelli** (1653-1713) was a famous Italian violinist and composer who spent much of his life working in Rome. He was one of the first to compose the concerto grosso, an early type of concerto, in which a small group of solo instruments is contrasted against the full orchestra. Corelli's twelve printed Concerti Grossi were instantly successful and widely imitated throughout Europe. There are eyewitness accounts of Corelli leading an orchestra of up to 150 players in one performance. The 'Largo' used here is from Op.6 No.1. The 'Pastorale' movement from Corelli's 'Christmas Concerto' (Op.6 No.8) is also well known.

*Bars 21-28 are written as a D.C. in the Pupil's Book.

The Lorelei   German

American Patrol   F.W. Meacham

18

Las Heras Beguine Pitts

Andante Mendelssohn

Fear No Danger   Purcell

This piece is a vocal duet from Purcell's opera 'Dido and Aeneas', written in London in 1689. This particular duet uses a musical form called a **rondo.** The first tune A returns twice later on at A2 and A3 . Two contrasting passages called 'episodes' (tunes B and C) separate the returns of the main tune A . So a rondo can be described as an **A B A C A** form.

Yellow Bird Calypso

Not too fast ($\quarternote$ = 100)

27

Peacherine Rag   Scott Joplin

Scott **Joplin** (1868-1917) was one of America's first black composers of Ragtime piano music. Ragtime music developed in the 1890's as an early type of jazz. The piano style of the day had developed a bouncing, left hand bass and an elaborate, syncopated melody line. Because it sounded as ragged as a torn cloth it was called 'ragged time', then 'ragtime'. Its effect was catching and it spread rapidly from honky-tonk bars into theatres, dancehalls and via sheet music and piano rolls into homes throughout America.

Joplin called his first rag 'The Maple Leaf Rag' after a club where he played piano in Sedalia, Missouri. Other popular rags by Joplin include 'The Entertainer', 'The Easy Winners' and 'Peacherine Rag', the first part of which is used here.

La Paloma   Yradier

Habanera from **Carmen**   Bizet

Rondo Mozart